MAXWELL GOES TO THE ZOO

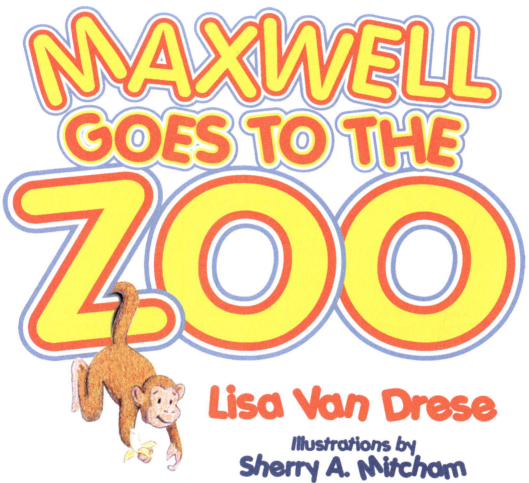

Lisa Van Drese

Illustrations by
Sherry A. Mitcham

Maxwell Goes to the Zoo
by Lisa Van Drese

Printed in the United States of America

ISBN 9781498478267

www.xulonpress.com

For my little love,
Maxwell

When Max woke up
he had no clue.
His mommy was taking him
to the zoo!

When Max got there
his eyes got wide.
There were so many animals
from side to side.

There were tigers, lions,
and monkeys, too.
What a grand idea
to go to the zoo!

Max grabbed
Mommy's hand and said,
"Let's go see!"

"Look at all of those birds
that can talk to me!"

Max loved the parrots,
so they went to take a peek.

They both laughed with delight when the birds started to speak.

They saw zebras, giraffes and crocodiles, too.

They even saw some cows that hollered out,
"Moo!"

Max fed handfuls of corn
to a goat named Fred,
While patting a big llama
on top of the head.

The snakes slithered about,
in their pen made of glass,

While the bunny rabbits pranced around in the grass.

They walked
all around
the zoo that day.

Max was so sorry they could not stay.

Mommy told him that Daddy
would love the story of the zoo.
That way Daddy gets to go
along with us, too.

Max smiled and nodded,
because it was true to say.
Daddy always loved a story
of a very good day.

"Thanks for the day at the zoo!"
Max said with a grin,

"I'll tell Dad all about it
when he is tucking me in."

Lisa Van Drese

Lisa lives in Gladstone, Michigan with her husband, Doug. They have two children, Andréa and Maxwell. Lisa is the author of the articles, "My Son Maxwell" and "The Things I Have Learned" and is wrapping up her informational guide entitled, "Down syndrome: One Mother's Truth". She is a national advocate for all people with Down syndrome and stands firmly in the belief that every life has value.

Maxwell is a five year old little boy who was born with Down syndrome, which means that he has an extra copy of the 21st chromosome. Max enjoys the same things that his typically developing peers do, but it may take him a bit longer to accomplish them. Max has taught us all so much and has brought his family closer in the process. *Maxwell Goes to the Zoo* is a tribute to Max and every other overachiever who just happens to rock an extra chromosome!

Sherry A. Mitcham

Sherry is a graphic designer and self-taught colored pencil artist living in Fayetteville, Georgia with her husband, Bill, and cockerpoo, Chloe.

Other titles Sherry has illustrated include *The Chipmunk Family Odyssey* by Linda Silva, Sandy McClure and Margie Mangham, *Things I Ponder* by Sandy McClure, and *I Love You More Than More* by Richard Swann Dalhberg.

CPSIA information can be obtained
at www.ICGtesting.com
Printed in the USA
LVOW02s1943200916

505475LV00002B/3/P